At the Bus Station

By Julia Jaske

2 I see drivers at the bus station.

I see buses at the bus station.

4 I see radios at the bus station.

I see mechanics at the bus station. 5

I see bags at the bus station.

I see windows at the bus station.

I see riders at the bus station.

I see maps at the bus station.

10 I see tickets at the bus station.

I see mirrors at the bus station.

12 I see seatbelts at the bus station.

I see cleaners at the bus station.

Word List

bus   mechanics   tickets

station   bags   mirrors

drivers   windows   seatbelts

buses   riders   cleaners

radios   maps

- I see drivers at the bus station.
- I see buses at the bus station.
- I see radios at the bus station.
- I see mechanics at the bus station.
- I see bags at the bus station.
- I see windows at the bus station.
- I see riders at the bus station.
- I see maps at the bus station.
- I see tickets at the bus station.
- I see mirrors at the bus station.
- I see seatbelts at the bus station.
- I see cleaners at the bus station.

CHERRY BLOSSOM PRESS

Published in the United States of America by Cherry Lake Publishing Group
Ann Arbor, Michigan
www.cherrylakepublishing.com

Book Designer: Keri Riley

Photo Credits: cover: © Baxtar/Shutterstock; page 1: © Zamrznuti tonovi/Shutterstock; page 2: © Africa Studio/Shutterstock; page 3: © Africa Studio/Shutterstock; page 4: © antoniodiaz/Shutterstock; page 5: © hedgehog94/Shutterstock; page 6: © Robert Przybysz/Shutterstock; page 7: © Olena Yakobchuk/Shutterstock; page 8: © Monkey Business Images/Shutterstock; page 9: © ChameleonsEye/Shutterstock; page 10: © VGstockstudio/Shutterstock; page 11: © Ground Picture/Shutterstock; page 12: © Pressmaster/Shutterstock; page 13: © hedgehog94/Shutterstock; page 14: © Mikbiz/Shutterstock

Note from publisher: Websites change regularly, and their future contents are outside of our control. Supervise children when conducting any recommended online searches for extended learning opportunities.

Cherry Blossom Press is an imprint of Cherry Lake Publishing Group.

Library of Congress Cataloging-in-Publication Data

Names: Jaske, Julia, author.
Title: At the bus station / written by Julia Jaske.
Description: Ann Arbor, Michigan : Cherry Blossom Press, 2023. | Series: In the community | Audience: Grades K-1 | Summary: "At the Bus Station explores the sights and sounds of the bus station. It covers people and objects found at the bus station. Uses the Whole Language approach to literacy, combining sight words and repetition to build recognition and confidence. Simple text makes reading these books easy and fun. Bold, colorful photographs that align directly with the text help readers with comprehension"— Provided by publisher.
Identifiers: LCCN 2023003188 | ISBN 9781668927175 (paperback) | ISBN 9781668929698 (ebook) | ISBN 9781668931172 (pdf)
Subjects: LCSH: Readers (Primary) | LCGFT: Readers (Publications).
Classification: LCC PE1119.2 .J358 2023 | DDC 428.6/2–dc23/eng/20230206
LC record available at https://lccn.loc.gov/2023003188

Printed in the United States of America
Corporate Graphics